I0844326

The Journey Inward: Discovering Your Own Truth

The Journey Inward: Discovering Your Own Truth
Copyright © 2023 by **Monday Farouq**
All rights reserved. No part of this publication may be reproduced, distributed, or transmitted in any form or by any means, including photocopying, recording, or other electronic or mechanical methods, without the prior written permission of the publisher, except in the case of brief quotations embodied in critical reviews and certain other noncommercial uses permitted by copyright law.

Table of Content

Introduction

The journey inward is a path many wish to traverse, yet few actually embark upon. It is a heroic undertaking of self-discovery - of excavating our buried truths, integrating our fragmented parts, and aligning our outer lives with our innermost values. This is the work of a lifetime, requiring courage, persistence and deep introspection.

As human beings, we often look outside ourselves for direction. We adopt others' expectations or seek validation through career, status and material gains. Yet inner harmony and fulfillment arises from a different source - from a deep knowledge of our true selves and a commitment to authentic living. As the ancient Greek aphorism declares, "Know thyself."

The Call to Adventure

There comes a time when the soul whispers that there must be more. More than the chameleon-like changing of selves to please others. More than the trophies lining the mantle but leaving the heart empty. This is the call to the adventure of self-discovery.

Like mythical heroes hearing the summons to an unknown quest, we feel both thrill and fear. Excitement at what we might discover beneath the surface, and trepidation about what we may confront should we dive deeper. But as Joseph Campbell wrote in *The Hero with a Thousand Faces*, "The adventure is always and everywhere the same...the dangerous passage of the threshold is a transit into a sphere of rebirth."

Such is the nature of the inward journey. By exploring the unmapped realm within, we inevitably encounter our shadows - those aspects of ourselves we have neglected, denied or repressed. The temptation is to turn away, back toward the safety of the known. Yet integrating these lost fragments holds the key to wholeness. As Carl Jung put it, "Those who look outside, dream. Those who look inside, awaken."

Traveling Companions

The path inward is unique to each of us, yet we need not walk alone. Throughout history, guides have shared their discoveries to encourage and support fellow explorers. The pages ahead synthesize such timeless wisdom to serve as a field guide for your adventure.

While the destination is ultimately yours to discover, these chapters provide trail markers for wayfinding, prompts for reflection, and advice for overcoming common obstacles. Think of this book as a conversation with a fellow sojourner - one further along, but still learning. A companion who says not "follow in my footsteps," but rather, "here are some tools I found useful - now go and scout your own trail."

Mapping the Terrain

Our inner landscape is vast and complex, its topography shaped by a lifetime of experiences both beautiful and painful. Navigating this terrain requires a variety of skills and perspectives:

The Cultivation of Stillness

Much like turbulent water obscures the riverbed, the noise and busyness of day-to-day life can make it difficult to peer beneath the surface thoughts and feelings flowing through our conscious minds. Practices for achieving inner stillness - such as meditation, journaling and time in nature - provide clarity for self-examination.

Sifting Through Layers

We are comprised of many layers, including temperament we were born with, formative experiences, emotional wounds, belief systems, roles we inhabit and more. Sorting through these strata reveals much about our inner constitution and psychological motivations.

Examining Relationships

Our interactions with others provide mirrors into our inner worlds. Observing how we relate reveals our emotional triggers and patterns, blind spots and latent potentials waiting to emerge.

Integrating Duality

Rather than being unified, we often feel conflicted - wanting to be selfless while also craving self-care, for example. Exploring seeming contradictions teaches us to embrace and integrate our multidimensionality.

Aligning with Purpose

As we come to know ourselves more deeply, we can craft an outward life that resonates with our inner truths. Making choices guided by our soul's wisdom rather than external pressures leads to fulfillment.

Practicing Presence

This journey unfolds in the here and now. While self-discovery requires looking back and peering forward, presence grounds us in each moment. Setting intentions, tuning into our senses and silencing self-judgment keeps us centered in the only time that truly exists - this instant.

An Unfolding Story

Who we are is neither static or definitive. Our inner and outer worlds are in constant interplay, mirrors that shift in reflection of each other. In sitting with ourselves - our feelings, beliefs, contradictions, fears and dreams - we invite more of our potential to unfold, like flowers thirsty for sunlight.

This book is not meant to crystallize a single truth, but rather kindle a spirit of curiosity, compassion and courage. May the questions posed stir more questions. May sharing vulnerability help ease the sense of isolation. And may you feel emboldened, at every step of your journey, to listen within. For as Rainer Maria Rilke wrote:

I beg you, to have patience with everything unresolved in your heart and to try to love the questions themselves as if they were locked rooms or books written in a very foreign language. Don't search for the answers, which could not be given to you now, because you would not be able to live them. And the point is to live everything. Live the questions now. Perhaps then, someday far in the future, you will gradually, without even noticing it, live your way into the answer.

With this spirit of discovery, let us begin...

Chapter 1: Preparing for the Journey Within

The inward odyssey requires preparation, both logistical and psychological. This chapter explores strategies for creating space, attuning the mind, and overcoming common obstacles at the outset of our shared path.

Making Space

The din of daily responsibilities echoes loudly, demanding our attention. We feel constantly busy, pulled in countless directions. This leaves little energy to focus inward. To amplify the quiet inner voice, we must first turn down the volume on the outer noise.

Retreating Into Silence

Lengthy silent retreats may seem intimidating for the uninitiated explorer. But even small doses of silence can recalibrate the mind. Wake up 30 minutes earlier than normal and sit quietly, observing your thoughts without reacting. Take a silent walk around the block. Turn off screens, music and conversation for an evening.

As we get accustomed to silence, its gifts become apparent. The space for reflection and connection with oneself it provides. The insights that arise when we stop distracting ourselves. Silence cleanses the doors of perception, opening pathways to wisdom within.

Creating Space in Your Calendar

Busyness is often less about having too much to do than about lack of boundaries. We say yes to every request and commitment, leaving no blanks in the calendar to wander inner landscapes.

Be intentional about scheduling self-reflection. Book regular appointments with yourself - perhaps an hour three mornings a week

- and protect that time, just as you would an important meeting. Use it to meditate, journal, take a quiet walk or simply sit.

At first, it may feel selfish or indulgent. In truth, filling your cup is critical to have energy and presence for others. Remind loved ones this time is sacred for you.

Alternatives to Mindless Scrolling

We frequently fritter away spare moments scrolling social media or idly browsing - quick dopamine hits that train the mind in distraction. Replace these with introspective activities.

Keep a journal by the couch to record thoughts. Designate reading time to learn rather than skim. Go outside and pause to observe nature. The minutes wasted in distraction add up, while intentional use of downtime adds depth.

Life's richness is unlocked in stillness, not speed. Be here now, rather than letting technology yank you elsewhere. The journey inward requires presence of mind, not just presence of body.

Immersing In Nature

Nature's tranquility has a healing effect on the harried soul. Time spent wandering forests, lying in fields or meandering coastlines eases anxiety and tunes us to more essential frequencies.

Studies show that being in nature restores focus, reduces stress hormones, improves mood and boosts creativity by as much as 50 percent. Build regular outdoor time into your schedule, leaving devices behind to fully unplug.

Immerse all your senses - sight, smell, sound, touch, taste. Hike to a remote waterfall to be awe-struck by its thunderous power. Stand atop a mountain, inhaling crisp air scented with pine, to gain perspective. Float in a placid lake, embraced by its calm. Nature is the ultimate mindfulness practice.

Adopting Beginner's Mind

In preparing for inner exploration, it is wise to let go of preconceptions. Beginner's mind offers a lens of openness and curiosity critical for discovery.

Acknowledging How Little We Know

We assume we know ourselves thoroughly. Yet there are endless depths within - life experiences, patterns, wounds and wisdom buried under the visible surface. The inward journey is an ever-deepening spiral; wherever we are is just a stopping point on the path, not the destination.

Those who think they have nothing left to learn set the firmest boundaries on growth. Know you have only glimpsed a sliver thus far. There are vistas and valleys yet ahead to explore.

Listening Without Judgment

Imagine encountering your sensations, emotions and thoughts for the very first time. How would you receive them if not colored by past reactions?

Beginner's mind is the practice of listening within without judgment. Let what arises within you be neither good nor bad, wise nor foolish. Observe with neutrality as a phenomenon passes through awareness. This allows nuances and subtleties to emerge.

Suspend judgment long enough to understand. Analysis often obscures truth.

The Illusion of Objectivity

We believe we see the world exactly as it is. But perception inevitably passes through the lens of our conditioning - our experiences, biases, fears. two people can witness the same event yet walk away with opposite interpretations.

Your inner landscape is similarly filtered. Beginner's mind recognizes no observation is truly objective. Be open to perspectives clashing with your own. Hold truths lightly, as a finger pointing at the moon.

Childlike Curiosity

Children model beginner's mind. They explore the world with awe and wonder, unhindered by preconceptions of what is possible. Each moment overflows with potential.

Cultivate such curiosity about your inner world. Bring a sense of adventure. Regard sensations and emotions as phenomena to be explored, not reactions to suppress or indulge. You are on safari in the jungle of your psyche. What surprising creatures might cross your path?

This spirit of fascination relaxes self-judgment. You become a devoted student of yourself, eager for each glimpse within. Progress flows naturally.

Moving Past Resistance

With intention and preparation, you are ready to venture inward. But the mind resists this descent; it fears unraveling its tight grip of control. Be gentle yet persistent in coaxing it forward.

Witnessing Your Avoidance

The initial phase of most journeys features unexpected delays - missing passport, flight delay, traffic jam. Similarly, when preparing the inner journey, we unconsciously create obstacles.

Note when your mind attempts escape or distraction. "I'll just check email first..." "I'm too sleepy to meditate now." These delay tactics reveal resistance. But by noticing them, we deny them power. Observe the impulse without following it.

Getting lost is part of the process. With compassion, continue nudging yourself forward.

Lean Into Discomfort

Exploring inner realms often feels uncomfortable. We confront shame, guilt, anger and denial; the effort of interrogating our own psyche challenges and drains. This discomfort causes retreat to the familiar.

Yet leaning into difficulty prompts growth. Astronauts experience the "overview effect" - a profound shift in worldview - only from pushing through atmosphere's friction to reach space.

When discomfort arises, pause to breathe rather than reacting. Then gently deepen your focus. Progress lives on the other side of resistance.

Persistence Through Plateaus

Mountaintops are thrilling, but ascending requires persevering through plateaus - those stretches where the path levels out and scenery remains unchanged.

Inner development is similar. We have breakthrough moments of self-realization. But we spend more time gradually cultivating clarity through repetition - regular reflection, mindfulness, journaling.

Plateaus test commitment. Will we keep trekking with no tangible gain in sight? But just when it seems futile, the path tilts skyward once again. And we are propelled higher for having trudged mindfully through the flatlands.

The Light of Awareness

Our inner shadow exerts strong gravitational pull backwards into old thought patterns and behaviors. But conscious awareness has even greater power - that of a black hole swallowing darkness as it unfurls an era's final stars.

Shining awareness's light helps relinquish resistance. Notice self-sabotaging thoughts but refuse to engage them. Remain anchored in the breath. Return again and again to beginner's mind.

With care and wisdom, you are ready to cross the threshold and continue the journey within.

Tuning the Inner Instrument

Think of your mind as a complex instrument requiring tuning and warm up. Certain practices help hone its receptivity before diving inward. Just as athletes stretch muscles and musicians run scales, preparing consciousness readies us to access subtler frequencies.

Centering In the Body

Our sense of self lives primarily in the head. But the journey inward progresses through expanding awareness to include the entire body.

Make time daily to "drop down" into the body. Sit quietly and feel the points of contact with the floor and chair. Sense your clothes on your skin. Tune into the breath's movement through your chest. Take a slow walk mindfully noticing your feet touching the ground.

Getting grounded in physical sensations connects you with the present moment - the only point from which to access inner truth. Thoughts can lead astray. The body anchors you in what is.

Breathwork

Breath awareness is core to meditation traditions for good reason. Breath is the flywheel powering the mind-body connection. With focused attention on the inhale and exhale, the engine of the nervous system downshifts to a more relaxed pace.

Use breathwork to initiate reflection sessions. Sit comfortably. Close your eyes. Take a few deep belly breaths. Lengthen and soften as you exhale. When attention wanders, gently return to the breath.

Even a few minutes of conscious breathing triggers a cascade of benefits - slowed heart rate, lower cortisol, increased Alpha and Theta brainwave activity associated with wakeful relaxation. It signals to the mind and body that stillness is safe.

Priming with Uplifting Media

Just as you might listen to a rousing song before exercising, curating a playlist of inspirational videos, podcasts or texts can spark motivation for inner progress.

Seek out authors or speakers who empower your growth - those that challenge assumptions but ultimately leave you feeling hopeful about the human experience. Their voices can penetrate internal resistance and open windows to let the refreshing breeze of new perspectives enter.

Let affirming media be the wind lifting the sails of your imagination toward greater inner discovery. But listen critically, and ultimately use their words only to propel you deeper within your own truth.

The inward odyssey is ultimately one of self-reliance. External voices inspire but cannot take the journey for you. After garnering wisdom from others, sail forth to encounter your distinct inner sea.

Committing To The Path

With preparation complete, what remains is declaring your intention - ceremonially crossing the threshold into new territory. This final act of commitment consecrates the journey.

Voicing Your Intention

Private intentions silently dissipate, starved of the momentum that comes from declaration. Voice yours aloud. Share with someone supportive or state in a journal:

I am ready for the journey of self-discovery. I welcome the challenges and gifts this exploration will bring. I commit to probing my inner depths with courage and compassion. May my eyes be open, my heart vulnerable and my mind beginner's mind. Let this be my pilgrimage to live with greater purpose and fulfillment.

Hearing your own voice ignites belief. If hesitancy remains, rewrite your intention until it resonates. But commit the final version to memory, returning when doubts arise.

Ritualizing the Beginning

Mindfully demarcate the transition into new terrain. Enact a personal ritual signifying your embarkation - light a candle and sit in contemplation, take a meditative walk in nature, create an altar with inspiring photos and quotes.

Rituals provide structure and meaning to abstraction. Visibly recognize your passage across the threshold into inner depths. Allow reverence and gratitude to fill you. Even small ceremonies solidify intentions into reality.

Surrender and Self-Trust

Ultimately, the journey within requires surrender - of control, certainty, comfort. We must relinquish the familiar to encounter the new. Deeper truth awaits beneath our stories. But accessing it means surrendering attachment to the ego's narratives.

This is not passive surrender, but rather active trust - in the intelligence of our deepest self. By relaxing the constant commandeering of the conscious mind, we permit penetration to more expansive regions of knowledge within.

Commit now to trusting the unfolding journey. Inner richness appears once we quiet the insistence on predictability. You are ready to embark. So let go of outcomes, open your heart, and begin...

Chapter 2: Exploring Your Inner Landscape

With intention set and mind open, we now begin surveying the terrain within. This chapter provides guidance for navigating the many dimensions of your inner world - its emotional currents, mental topography and hidden caverns awaiting illumination.

Tuning Into Your Emotions

Emotions are powerful weather systems shaping our inner landscape. But often we tune them out, leaving important data undiscovered. Learning their language provides guidance for growth.

From Reactivity to Curiosity

We are conditioned to judge emotions as good or bad, so we cling to ones like joy while rejecting anger or sadness. But reacting to emotions often exacerbates them, like attempting to smooth a pond's ripples with forceful swipes - you just create more distortion.

Instead, adopt beginner's mind. Perceive each emotion as a phenomenon to greet with curiosity. Ask, "Why has this arisen? What is it trying to show me?"

Tune into its physical manifestation in your body - anger might be hot tension in the hands. Sadness, a hollowness in the chest. Observe without immediately reacting.

Identifying Core Feelings

Uncomfortable emotions usually conceal more vulnerable core feelings. Anger shields hurt. Bitterness protects longing. Cynicism defends hope. Peel away those outer layers to uncover what lies beneath.

Sit quietly with the emotion until its edges soften. Sense into it with compassion. Ask, "If this anger could speak, what would it say? What is it protecting?"

Naming the true feeling dissipates its intensity. Acknowledging pain transforms it into wisdom. GiveUnderstanding brings relief where judgment created contraction.

Catharsis Through Expression

Suppressed emotions accumulate like sediment in a stagnant pond. Finding healthy release prevents toxicity.

Catharsis can take many forms. Physical activity, crying or emotional outbursts discharge psychic tension. Talking with trusted listeners names feelings, dispelling their power. Creative expression channels intensity into art, writing or music.

Choose practices aligning with your temperament. Introverts prefer journaling, extroverts group sharing. When emotions feel flammable, vigorous exercise shifts that fire into motion.

Examining Your Beliefs

Our inner world is shaped by core beliefs - the mental models and assumptions through which we interpret reality. Some originate within, while others were inherited from family, culture or religion. Scrutinizing their validity liberates perception.

Where Beliefs Come From

Reflect on the key beliefs governing your life, like views around career, relationships, self-worth. Where did those ideas come from originally? Were they adopted unconsciously, or did you consciously choose them?

Our worldviews are profoundly shaped by early experiences, especially with caregivers. Messages absorbed in childhood become ingrained subconsciously. Shining awareness here helps dismantle limiting legacies.

Beliefs hastily adopted from society or religion also realign when exposed. Ideas that do not resonate with your considered perspective can be discarded.

Questioning Inherited Views

Examine any belief you have clung to without real analysis. Does it truly align with your values and understanding? Ask repeatedly, "Is this absolutely true?" Smash it open and test its veracity.

Stay alert to cognitive dissonance - when your actions conflict with your professed beliefs. This reveals shadow aspects and hidden judgements needing integration.

Subject even cherished convictions to scrutiny. As the philosopher Nietzche declared, "The most dangerous of errors is great truths held as prejudices." Remaining fluid keeps your inner sea from becoming a stagnant pool.

Discerning Empowering Beliefs

First inspect beliefs skeptically to clear space for empowering ones. Then carefully curate and reinforce those that expand, uplift and illuminate.

Affirmations work when sufficiently specific. Rather than "I am worthy," declare "I forgive myself for past mistakes and know I am worthy of love exactly as I am." Also affirm others' worth to elevate the collective.

Consciously seed your inner landscape with intentions. Repeating them anchors new patterns, just as water smooths stones.

Identifying Inner Conflict

We often feel torn inwardly. One part of us seeks adventure, another craves stability. We desire both intimacy and freedom. Multiple selves compete for control.

The catharsis of acknowledging duality opens space to integrate differences. Let's explore some key inner divides.

The Inner Critic vs Inner Wisdom

These two figures sit on our shoulders, voices contradicting each other. The critic admonishes and circulates fears. Wisdom emanates love and rational calm.

When receiving criticism, ask, "Is this wisdom or just harsh judgment?" Externally voiced criticism also echoes messages we tell ourselves. Shifting those inner narratives transforms self-talk.

Thank the critic for trying to keep you safe, but begin listening more to gentle wisdom. Apply criticism's energy toward growth rather than self-blame.

Resistance vs Allowing

One part of us fears change, clinging to comfort and identity. But another part yearns for growth. This tension manifests in everything from everyday choices to major life transitions.

When resistance arises, recognize its protective intention. But then affirm that you are ready for the next phase of expansion. Meeting resistance with compassion rather than anger dissolves its grip.

Logic vs Intuition

The rational mind values predictability; intuition leaps to unseen possibilities. Both offer gifts, so we don't need to choose one over the other.

Left-brain logic is ordered and analytical. But it also confines vision. Intuition spots connections that elude linear thinking. We integrate these modes through dialogue between them.

Masculine vs Feminine

These primal energies express themselves both within ourselves and collectively. The masculine pursues goals. The feminine nurtures process. Together they dance creatively.

Embrace the full spectrum. For women, cultivate leadership and self-authority (masculine). For men, develop receptivity, patience and collaboration (feminine). Integrating both builds wisdom.

Light vs Shadow

The most central yet difficult inner divide exists between disowned aspects of ourselves and who we believe ourselves to be. But denying shadow only gives it power.

Owning our mixed human nature brings forgiveness for faults, reducing their control over us. The journey within is really a path of shadow integration. We will continue this work of reconciliation.

For now, notice where you feel inner fragmentation. Hold these contradictory selves with empathy. Their unity reveals itself in time through spiritual alchemy.

Plumbing Your Psychological Depths

Having surveyed landscape revealed by the conscious mind, we now seek entry to the ocean of the unconscious - that vast repository of memories, wounds, desires and buried potentialities beneath awareness. Diving here retrieves riches.

Working with Dreams

In sleep, the ego's constraint loosens, permitting symbols of the unconscious to rise to the surface. Recalling dreams immediately upon waking and recording them accesses this untamed source of guidance.

Unlike the literal constructs of the rational mind, dreams speak in poetry, riddles and puns. By exploring meanings behind motifs, narrative patterns and emotional tones, insight emerges. Dreams connect us to lost parts of ourselves.

Exploring Synchronicity

Humans cling desperately to notions of a controllable, mechanical universe. But the inner mystic perceives divine designs - fateful connections and messages whispered to us through metaphor.

Pay attention to coincidences and omens. Reflect on what they reveal about your path ahead. Intuition speaks through synchronicity. Open your eyes to its guidance all around you.

Entering Creative Flow

Flow states transcend ego and unlock genius within. In music, sport, art or writing, we slip into timelessness, functioning as a vessel for inspiration beyond our normal capacity.

Through practicing creative expression and surrendering fixed expectations, we gain access to this magical realm of play and imagination. In flow, insights seem summoned from some eternal Source.

Accessing Your Inner Oracle

Cultures across history have used oracles - mediums tapping universal wisdom - in shaping decisions. Consider your deepest intuition an inner oracle. How might you access its prescience?

Try posing a dilemma aloud, then quieting your mind to receive counsel. Go for a walk allowing solutions to surface spontaneously. Attune to non-verbal cues - your body and emotions contain wisdom. Trusting inner sight unfolds intuition's wings.

Mapping Your Mental Topography

Having surveyed your inner world's depths, let's map its terrain by tracing mental habits and processes. This awareness enables rewiring.

Observing Thought Patterns

Notice your thought patterns without judgment. Tally how often certain themes arise. Do the same thoughts replay on loop? Does negativity outweigh positivity? Which situations activate anger or anxiety?

Mapping your cognitive landscape this way builds self-awareness. You might uncover cycles tied to certain mood states. Recognition alone can dissolve their power.

Catching Negative Bias

Due to evolutionary survival instincts, the mind is wired to accentuate negatives. One hundred positive events can be outweighed cognitively by one negative one.

Counter this by consciously catching positives. Keep a daily gratitude journal. Log kind acts. Reflect on what went well before bed. Give compliments.

We see what we look for. Training your mind's eye toward the light manifests more light.

Witnessing the Commentary

Much thinking amounts to meaningless internal commentary. We constantly judge circumstances, others and ourselves - an inner sportscaster analyzing each moment.

Notice when the voice of commentary arises. Try imagining it as a radio you can turn down. Decline to engage every passing thought. Rest as the impartial witness and thoughts lose their audience.

Naming the Storyteller

Beneath commentary lives the storyteller, who shapes identity by crafting narratives about your life. "I'm the victim here" or "I'll never succeed because..." This voice imposes labels limiting your potential.

Don't suppress stories, just recognize their subjectivity. Label it "story" and bow out. Say, "There goes the storyteller again, doing his thing." Naming this voice diffuses its power to own you.

Know your inner topography without being defined by it. As aware observer, you are larger than any passing thought. From this place of sovereignty, you are ready to intentionally remap your mental landscape toward wisdom.

Integrating Learning

This initial survey of your inner realm revealed much about its contours. Before proceeding further, pause to reflect.

Review Your Discoveries

Revisit notes from exploration so far. What insights about your emotional patterns, beliefs, conflicts and mental habits arose? Consider keeping an inner map like a sketch artist, detailing key features to re-examine later.

Highlight areas where shadow integration is needed - childhood conditioning limiting you now, destructive thought cycles, polarities causing distress. Our remaining trek will traverse these lands, so outline the terrain.

Appreciate Your Progress

The mind believes enlightenment will arrive in a burst, like a flash flood forever altering the valley. But in truth, it accrues slowly, like water smoothing stones. Each act of self-study shapes the psyche's edges incrementally.

Rather than judging yourself for not reaching a goal, appreciate effects of small steps. Reflecting for ten minutes strengthens awareness, making possible future 20-minute sits. Each look inward expands perception.

Assimilate Learning

For inner exploration to manifest outwardly, we must fully embody lessons, translating insight into action. Keep a "to practice" list. Revisit it often to check you are living what you learn.

Wisdom unapplied has little worth. Let truth change not just ideas, but behaviors. Integrate light until you become light, radiating love's frequency in each moment.

The journey continues, my friend. Onward we travel, into lands of shadow, where gold is found.

Chapter 3: Integrating Your Shadow Self

The notion of "shadow work" has entered mainstream but remains murky. This chapter provides concrete guidance for befriending your shadows - reclaiming and integrating the disowned aspects of your psyche.

What is "Shadow"?

Our ego, insecure about its constructed identity, bans parts of ourselves deemed dangerous or unflattering. But they don't disappear - they are suppressed into the unconscious as our "shadow."

The shadow comprises trauma we deny, qualities judged as shameful, authentic desires buried under "shoulds." We project this darkness onto others, fearing it internally. But embracing shadow is central to becoming whole.

Let's demystify this process through examples, practices and courageous self-examination. There are astonishing gifts found only in the dark.

Excavating Your Wounds

Painful memories, if left unprocessed, create energetic blockages preventing growth. Clearing this trauma is arduous but essential work.

Identifying Wounds

Reflect on periods of your life associated with grief, shame or rejection. Perhaps childhood losses, bullying, abusive relationships or addiction. Consider major regrets still carrying weight.

Feel into these memories with compassion. Locate where their pain continues to store in your body. Offer them space to surface after years of suppression.

Allowing Catharsis

Now, dialogue with these wounded parts of yourself, speaking from your highest and most loving self: "You endured things no child should. You did nothing to deserve this pain. I am here for you now." Feel repressed emotions arise, wash through you and release. Share your story with trusted listeners. Speak your unspoken truths, shedding their poison.

Rewriting Your Story

Wounds whisper limiting stories about ourselves that persist decades later. "I am unlovable, worthless, stupid..."

Pen a new narrative to dismantle these. Honor the wisdom gained from hardship without allowing victimhood. Let this chapter in your life story close so a new one can begin.

Unburdening To Spirit

Prayer, meditation or ritual connects us to an energy greater than our individual pain. Surrendering ego allows us to purge burdens as light passes through us.

Imagine your higher self or a divine being absorbing your suffering into their infinite compassion. Feel the cords loosening and dissolving. Breathe gratitude for being made new.

Exploring Your Dark Desires

Desire is the shadow's playground. Yet repressing it causes distortion, while accepting it brings freedom.

Acknowledging Forbidden Wanting

Desire's force often provokes repression - cravings for wealth, attention, substances or carnal pleasures seem "sinful." But banning them from consciousness inflates their power.

Admitting forbidden desires demystifies them. Say aloud, even just in journaling: "Part of me craves fame, sexual conquests or massive financial gain." Simply voicing it releases a valve of pressure.

Indulging Healthily

A small dose of indulgence prevents repression from rebounding explosively. Allow yourself measured satisfaction of cravings without shame.

Be mindful as you experience brief sensual or material pleasures. Indulging consciously prevents addiction and discharged desire's magnetism.

Moderation aligns us with divine will - neither extreme austerity nor recklessness, but the middle way. Know all desires arise from primal longing for wholeness. Channel this life force wisely.

Aligning with Your Higher Purpose

The ultimate solution for excess desire is redirecting it toward purpose. Our deepest hunger can only be filled by our unique soul mission.

When craving arises, pause and ask, "How might this impulse be channeling my creative potential? What dream is this hunger really for?" Then take inspired action.

Working with Sexual Shadow

Sexuality often inhabits the deepest recesses of shadow, resulting in shame, repression or obsession. But its sacred essence is a potent creative force.

Be radically honest with yourself about your desires. Allow hidden parts of your erotic nature to reveal themselves without judgment. Then channel this animating energy into art, spirituality or connections founded on love, not ego.

Examining Your Addictions

Addictions promise refuge yet entrap us. But we can break their hold through courage and accountability.

Honest Self-Appraisal

Admitting addiction's grip requires ruthless honesty. Keeping secrets perpetuates the cycle. Ask trusted friends for feedback. Talk to a counselor or recovery group to dismantle denial.

Shine light on patterns over years, not days. Addiction's slippery nature tricks us as we move from one fixation to another. But repeatedly voicing truth aloud builds self-awareness and strength to change.

Discovering the Need Underneath

Explore what emotional void the addiction temporarily fills. Social anxiety? Depression? Childhood insecurity? Feel the underlying wounds addiction hides.

Healing means learning to meet unmet needs directly rather than through escape. Counseling, healthy social connections, inner child work, and lifestyle changes addressing root causes help erect your spine of self-reliance.

Committing to Accountability

Breaking addiction requires rigor and support. Commit to recovery groups, counseling, detox, rehab or whatever your condition requires. Communicate openly with allies holding you accountable.

Write down commitment vows and place them where you will see them when cravings strike. Reread them as affirmations of self-trust. Redemption lies ahead, however long the road.

Exploring Your Darker Emotions

We repress emotions deemed negative. But welcoming them with courage is the road to wholeness.

Sensing into Envy and Jealousy

Few emotions cause more anguish than envy toward others' success or possessions. Jealousy inflicts similar torment regarding relationships. Both signal disconnection from your true gifts.

Rather than banishing the feelings, sit with them. Ask "What unmet need are these pointing to in me? What dream do I feel deprived of?" Then take one small step toward manifesting that gift or calling. Even writing out your ideal vision starts to dissolve envy's acidic corrosion.

Embracing Sadness and Grief

Cultures imbued with "toxic positivity" classify sadness as weakness. But grieving is a sacred rite of passage. Only by fully feeling loss can you re-emerge renewed.

When bereft, do not cling feverishly to optimism. Allow waves of sorrow without shame. Cry out, wail, speak of death's injustice. In time, tears cleanse the wounded soul. You will breathe again without each inhalation stinging.

Making Friends With Your Anger

Anger drinks bitterness and spews poison - unless digested through compassion. Suppressing it causes disease, but examining anger's messages transforms it into wisdom.

Consider each flare up an invitation to know yourself more deeply. Ask calmly, "What fear or hurt is causing this anger? What is it trying to protect or communicate?" Listen, then respond thoughtfully. Anger, thanked for warning of issues needing attention, loses its virulence. We make an ally where there once was an aggressor.

Letting In Appropriate Darkness

Light cannot penetrate where we ban all shadows. Stop fearing your full range of human emotions as existential threats. Trust in the indestructible diamond essence of the Self.

Allow natural cycles of joy, grief, laughter, rage and more without judgment when appropriate. No feeling fully expressed will wash you away. Wisdom integrates all seasons into a beautiful whole.

Transmuting Shame

Shame often becomes embedded deep in the psyche, secretly influencing our identity. Shedding this dead skin of unworthiness requires brutal honesty and courage.

Pinpointing Your Shames

What experiences or parts of yourself do you try desperately to hide? Addictions? Body shame? Selfish impulses?

Speak or journal about these shadows in detail. Describe exactly what you fear being exposed. This confession releases their grip. Your words hold no weight but the power you grant them.

Separating Deeds From Identity

Shame conflates our errors with our being. But no action defines your totality. Admit mistakes without global self-judgment.

Say aloud: "I made a hurtful choice, but that does not mean I am evil. My errors do not preclude future kindness." Disaggregating deeds from self is immensely liberating.

We are all imperfect angels, neither destined for sainthood nor damned to live as monsters. Remember this.

Cultivating Self-Compassion

Replace shaming self-talk with compassion. Imagine advising your most beloved friend in a similar situation. You would likely offer loving wisdom, not scorn. Apply this same grace to yourself.

Repeating phrases like "May I be happy. May I be peaceful. May I be free." begins to unwind shame's bands constricting the heart. Speak to yourself gently. You are worthy.

Excavating the Roots

Shame sunk its roots in childhood, when caretakers instilled a sense of deficiency through criticism, abuse or neglect.

Revisit these memories with mindfulness. Imagine nurturing your inner child exactly as they needed. Say to them, "You did nothing to warrant this shame. You deserve unconditional love." Feel old wounds begin to mend.

Integrating Your Inner Darkness

Shadow work is not about destroying any part of yourself, but rather reclaiming exiled aspects back into the light of self-compassion. Here are some final principles for befriending your darkness.

All Parts Have Value

Trust that every part of you serves an important purpose, even if you don't yet understand it. The most twisted parts hold great gifts once redeemed through wisdom. Be patient with the process of illumination.

Darkness is Light Misunderstood

Shadow is simply the blind spot of awareness. Darkness is not the enemy, but rather a lost fragment of sacred light not yet recognized as part of the greater whole. It seems evil only due to exclusion. But embraced, it reveals its brilliance.

Integration, Not Eradication

Don't seek to eliminate aspects of yourself, but rather acknowledge their role and redirect them positively. Anger becomes assertion. Lust transforms to passionate love. Greed's audacity fuels bold ambition.

All energy contains potential for greatness or destruction. Integrate and harness it wisely.

From Canyon to Canyon

The journey's climax approaches. We have explored peaks and valleys within, integrating opposites, transmuting flaws into blessings. But one final abyss remains - the one between individual consciousness and universal spirit. Our work now is bridging that canyon, tying personal truth to cosmic oneness.

Take heart, and let's continue ascending...

Chapter 4: Finding Your Inner Voice

With expanded self-knowledge comes clearer discernment of our inner voice - the wisdom flowing through us when ego quiets. This chapter explores ways to amplify this gentle guidance and override limiting mental patterns.

Quieting the Inner Critic

The saboteur within undermines through harsh criticism, fueling anxiety and perfectionism. Learning to override this voice is pivotal.

Noticing Its Impact

Start by observing just how frequently your inner critic comments, compares and condemns. Note when it pipes up and how it makes you feel.

Does self-judgment inspire excellence or paralyze you? Motivate or demean? Gathering data exposes the critic's limited usefulness. Much of its narrative distorts reality.

Diffusing Its Power

When you notice the critic attacking, consciously pause and interrupt the message. Say silently, "There's the critic again, doing its thing."

Creating space around the voice separates it from your identity. Name it as an autonomous entity, rather than your absolute truth. This diffuses its power over you.

Speaking Back With Compassion

Once you create distance from the critic, you can respond calmly without being shaken.

Thank the voice for trying to protect you, but explain there are better ways to catalyze growth. Use affirmations to counter its negativity. The critic loses volume when met with firm self-love.

Replacing Criticism with Encouragement

The critic berates to motivate, but actually fuels resistance. For every negative thought, consciously voice two positive ones. Focus on progress made rather than perceived imperfections.

Write encouraging notes to leave around your home. Set reminders to celebrate small wins. The soul responds to warmth, not coldness. With compassion, you outgrow the critic's narrow vision.

Building Self-Trust

As the critic's grip loosens, we cultivate trust in our inherent wisdom. But after years muting our inner voice, how do we discern its message?

Observing Your Track Record

Our intuitive voice is revealed through the trail of choices we've made. Reflect on past decisions where you acted on inner conviction versus external pressures. Consider which ones led to fulfillment.

Seeing how often intuition served you builds trust to follow it again. We have all acted from inner wisdom successfully, even if not the majority of time. Review enough evidence of this and self-trust blooms.

Noticing Whispers

Deep down, you've always known the next right step - instincts too subtle to be called a "voice," more like whispers. But hushed or hurried, we push them aside.

Start tuning into nudges urging you to call a friend, change jobs, leave a relationship, etc. Begin to honor impulses without demanding loud clarity. The soul speaks through whispers and whimpers as much as shouts.

Letting Go of Overcontrol

We distrust inner wisdom because it arises spontaneously, not on our carefully planned timeline. Relinquishing the need to control everything frees us to follow unexpected promptings.

Practice acting on intuition in low-risk scenarios - taking an unplanned detour, stopping into a store, exploring a new neighborhood. Then build trust to act on bold life guidance when it comes.

Honing Your Listening

As with a weak radio signal, it takes practice to isolate the faint sounds of inner wisdom amidst mental noise. But tuning in more intently reveals its constant presence.

Try novel forms of listening - recording yourself speaking on a topic then playing it back, having a written dialogue by hand, or just walking silently. As ego steps aside, truth steps forward.

Overriding Past Conditioning

Childhood imprints convinced us we were too sensitive, selfish or broken in some way. But we can consciously rewire self-beliefs.

Uncovering Your Core Stories

What central stories do you subconsciously tell yourself about your worth and abilities? Were they stories others imposed on you as a child that you internalized?

Shining light on these narratives robs them of control. Write down their messages so you can purposefully edit the scripts. Just articulating them releases their grip.

Rewriting Your Inner Monologue

Replace disempowering tapes with positive truths through repetition. On index cards, write affirmations contradicting old stories, i.e. "I am enough. I am safe and supported." Repeat these daily.

In time, nurturing self-talk overrides the harsh conditioning. Be patient with the process of reprogramming neural pathways. But stay persistent.

Separating Past From Present

Breathe deep to reconnect with your adult self, here and now. Recall that you are not helpless and trapped in childhood any longer, unless you allow your mind to time travel back there.

Bring full awareness to the present moment - your body, the sights and smells around you, the fact that you get to make choices. You severed the cord; your past has no power but what you grant it. This realization sets you free.

Allowing New Identity to Emerge

As old stories fade, a new sense of self will organically arise, just as spring growth pushes through melted snow. Affirm your readiness to move into this next chapter.

Shedding limiting roles creates space for truer identity to sprout and flourish. With curiosity, observe how your beliefs, values and self-image expand. Nurture what emerges. You are ready to be reborn.

Honoring Your Intuitions

Intuition provides a compass in the wilderness, pointing us toward truth when the mind alone cannot discern the way. Following intuition requires separating rational fear from wisdom.

Noticing Inner Cues

Intuition communicates through sensations, emotions, imagery and "coincidences." Attune to these signals.

Does a prospect you are considering elicit warmth or unease? Take note of passing mental pictures and metaphors. Synchronicities confirm inner promptings. Start recognizing intuition's language. Write down insights for clarity.

Differentiating From Anxiety

Ego generates false warnings out of base survival fears. Intuition steps in with steady guidance when the mind loses its grip.

Anxiety feels frantic and fixates on worst-case scenarios. Intuition is a calm inner knowing, neutral rather than emotional. Learn their distinct languages. You will grow to trust the still, small voice.

Taking Small Leaps of Faith

Rather than demanding total clarity, take incremental steps when intuition gently pulls you. Follow the trail of breadcrumbs.

Start with lower-risk actions like researching a potential career pivot or scheduling a difficult conversation. Once you feel guided support each time you listen and leap, faith builds.

Reaffirming Your Worthiness

We often ignore intuition's direction because of a belief we are undeserving or incapable. But your inner light would not guide you astray.

Remind yourself regularly that you are worthy of following your purpose. Repeat affirmations of your competence. Self-trust must be reinforced until it becomes second nature.

Trust in your heart's wisdom. It knows the way.

Discerning Core Values

With clearer inner sight comes realignment between your values and choices. Defining your ethics provides a blueprint for this.

Identifying Guiding Principles

What values shape your sense of purpose and ethics? Honesty? Justice? Community? Autonomy? Make a list of words capturing your core ideals.

Look for common themes. Do certain values like integrity arise repeatedly across life areas? Their prominence reveals their centrality in guiding you.

Affirming Priorities

Now narrow this list to just top 3-5 ethical pillars. These will focus your choices. Seek overlap between personal fulfillment and social contribution.

Turn selected principles into affirmations. "I live with integrity." "I work for the greater good." Post these reminders of what matters most and recite them when facing decisions.

Auditing Your Behaviors

Take an honest audit of how consistently your actions align with declared values. In what areas do you fall short?

Without judgment, note any discrepancies, such as valuing honesty but rarely speaking up. This self-awareness empowers you to close gaps between ideals and reality.

Adhering to Standards

Commit to making choices based on core values, rather than fleeting desires or convenience. Set standards aligned with ethics.

Establishing boundaries creates healthy self-restraint. If financial modesty is a value, cap frivolous purchases. If ecology matters to you, commit to vegetarianism. Clarifying values crystallizes how to live them.

Crafting an Inner Code

Defining a concise inner code synthesizes our principles and priorities into a creed guiding all choices. This daily touchstone keeps us aligned.

Distilling Your Wisdom

Study notes from inner exploration so far - key lessons, life purposes, realized truths. Capture these as concisely as possible.

Boil down wisdom into simple maxims. "Live openly." "Love deeply." "Speak truth with compassion." Distill insights into their essence, removing circumstantial details.

Choosing Your Words

Frame your code using language that resonates. Consider meaningful quotes and sacred verses as well as your own phrases.

Edit these passages like a poet seeking poetry. Craft succinct lines that penetrate directly to the heart. Profound truths require minimalist expression.

Writing Your Code

Synthesize selected words into a cohesive code with 5-10 maxims. Format it attractively on a small card you can carry.

Write your code by hand, feeling meanings enter more deeply than by typing. Read it slowly each morning and night to imprint it on your consciousness. Modify over time as your inner wisdom expands.

Putting Wisdom into Action

For your code to carry power, its principles must translate into daily practices and rituals. Identify 1-2 actions for each maxim.

A vow of patience could involve meditative breathing when frustrated. Speaking compassionately may mean listening generously before responding. Codes come alive through embodiment.

May this distillation of your soul's wisdom guide you through life's maze with clarity. You are ready now to live by your inner light.

Chapter 5: Aligning with Your True Self

With increased self-knowledge comes the work of integrating that wisdom into how we live. This chapter explores practices for aligning outer life and inner truth through authenticity, boundaries and mindful self-expression.

Living Authentically

Authenticity means honoring your emotions, needs and values despite external pressures. Constructing an identity around these core components allows sincere living.

Noticing When You Are Inauthentic

Reflect on situations where you hide truth to appease others - minimizing emotions, withholding opinions, allowing poor treatment, etc.

Also notice when you perform a socially-scripted role not fully aligned with your true nature. Make note of these moments of incongruity. Recognition is the first step toward realignment.

Owning Your Needs

Tune into needs you routinely ignore in order to accommodate others - the need for rest, personal space, quiet time alone, etc.

Prioritizing these does not make you selfish. Fill your own cup first so you can fully show up for relationships without depletion or resentment. Give yourself full permission to honor essential needs.

Voicing Your Perspective

Practice expressing your viewpoint, even if it contradicts the majority opinion. Speak calmly and thoughtfully, grounded in your experience and values.

You may be surprised how often others have secretly shared your minority view but were also afraid to voice it first. Your courage empowers them.

Aligning Appearance with Identity

Mindfully edit your appearance to better reflect inner truth rather than chasing trends. Adorn in ways resonating with your personality.

Those who feel most beautiful are not following but interpreting fashion in their own style. Let your clothing communicate your unique spirit. Authenticity always looks best.

Setting Healthy Boundaries

Essential to authenticity is establishing boundaries - rules defining treatment you accept versus behavior you won't tolerate. Kindly yet firmly enforce these to protect your energy.

Identifying Your Limits

Consider situations where people violate your boundaries through disrespect, criticism, dishonesty, etc. Make note of what feels unacceptable.

Also set personal boundaries around time management, work-life balance, when to say no, financial priorities and information sharing. Boundaries cultivate self-trust.

Communicating Your Boundaries

Calmly inform others when their actions overstep bounds, both in the moment and proactively if patterns exist. Be specific about desired changes.

If violations continue after fair warning, enact consequences - reduced contact, terminating friendships or employment, counseling. Healthy relationships require mutual respect.

Setting Time Boundaries

Protect your time and attention - limited resources easily drained. Determine how much you want to allot to work, family, self-care, etc. based on inner wisdom, not pressure.

Learn to say no to requests that exceed your bandwidth. Curate a schedule honoring your natural rhythms. You decide where your hours go.

Standing Firm in Values

Boundaries falter when we waver on ethics. Establish moral lines you refuse to cross, like lying, cheating, or compromising family time for work demands.

Train your mind to exclude certain choices completely rather than weighing them. This reduces stress and preserves integrity when pressured.

Taming the Ego

The ego - our sense of individual self - must eventually surrender to the wisdom of the higher Self. This letting go allows fuller expression of your divine potential.

Recognizing Ego's Voice

Notice when your inner monologue fixates on "I, me, mine" versus universal concerns. Ego maintains a constant commentary about how each event relates to your needs.

Catch yourself judging, clinging to desires, demanding outcomes cater to you. The ego's desires are insatiable. But you have the power to stop indulging its whims.

Accepting Your Role in the Universe

The ego wants everything to revolve around its drama. But events have little to do with you specifically. Shift from main character mindset to understanding your small role in the cosmic play.

Surrender self-centered thinking and attachment to results. Make choices based on aligning with divine order rather than satisfying the ego. This reduces suffering.

Becoming the Observer

Retrain focus from your narrow story to the broader universe. Cultivate witness consciousness - observing ego's demands with detached compassion, rather than identifying with them.

Note the ego's antics and fears non-judgmentally. "There goes ego again, wanting things its way." Without engaging or judging, the ego's volume diminishes.

Letting Spirit Lead

Abandon trying to meticulously plan life rather than allowing higher power to guide you. Adapt an attitude of open receptivity.

Follow intuitive nudges down unexpected but aligned paths. Say "yes" to invitations to growth. Your soul knows the way; trust its wisdom over ego's desire for control.

Expressing Your Authentic Self

Suppressing our personality creates disconnection from self. But exercising creative outlets for honest self-expression fosters empowerment.

Exploring Your Dormant Gifts

What creative talents gave you joy as a child but were discouraged? Dance? Singing? Painting? Poetry? Make a list, then commit to exploring them.

Schedule time to experiment with these neglected parts of yourself without judgment. Your soul longs to activate these latent gifts. Let their playfulness heal and reconnect you.

Moving Your Body Authentically

Notice how you restrict your body's natural movement due to self-consciousness - crossing legs, hunching shoulders, tightly clutching arms.

Practice unwinding by dancing freely when alone, shaking limbs loose, walking with shoulders back. Moving in ways unique to you boosts energy and creative flow.

Writing Your Authentic Story

Journaling empowers self-discovery, but crafting your life's story as a narrative arc clarifies understanding of your journey.

Detail the major plot points and themes. Recall pivotal moments, the origin of beliefs and quirks, your heroic qualities. Weaving your memories into a manuscript illuminates purpose.

Finding Your Medium

Experiment with mediums like photography, pottery, poetry, singing, rap, stand-up comedy. Unconventional creative outlets bypass our inner critic and reveal truths.

Playfully subvert your standard forms of expression. If you're a banker, try painting. Attempt comedy. Disrupting patterns jars something beautiful loose. Follow what enlivens you.

Sculpting Your Environment

Since our surroundings profoundly impact well-being, consciously curating your environment nurtures alignment with your highest self.

Removing Energy Drains

Examine your living and working spaces. What objects or elements subtly drain your spirit? Items from old chapters holding expired meaning? Photos of lost loved ones causing pain?

Mindfully edit your habitat. Donate or discard forgotten objects obscuring your present-moment clarity. Sometimes renewal requires making space.

Bringing in Inspiration

Now fill your spaces with energy-giving elements - artwork, quotes, photos, books, music, plants, and colors that uplift and inspire you.

You might add vision boards with clippings of goals, natural crystals emitting positive vibrations, essential oils elevating mood, sage for cleansing stuck energies. Mindfully curate beauty.

Designing Ideal Work & Living Spaces

Make notes on your optimal environment if resources were unlimited. What would nourish productivity, relaxation, creativity and contentment in your ideal workspace and home?

Begin incrementally upgrading aspects of current spaces to align with this vision. Even subtle tweaks towards your values-based oasis send ripples through consciousness.

Choosing Community Carefully

Just as physical space impacts you, closely consider who you invite into emotional and mental space. Limit time with those who drain energy.

Seek out mutual uplifting friendships. Surround yourself with those committed to growth, optimism and empowerment. Your vibe determines your tribe. Choose company elevating your vibration.

The quest of aligning inner and outer takes constant patience and perseverance. But each act of authenticity builds integrity and self-trust. You walk your path with more lightness having unburdened what does not serve your spirit. Onward...

Chapter 6: Charting Your Inner Path

With expanded self-knowledge comes clearer discernment of life purpose. This chapter explores practices for aligning daily choices with soulful vision through intention-setting, mindful productivity, and defining success on your own terms.

Clarifying Core Intentions

Intentions provide a compass bearing between inner truth and external expression. Articulating yours channels energy toward manifesting your highest vision.

Connecting with Your Destiny

Consider your unique talents, passions and values. If you had unlimited time and resources, what would you dedicate your energies to creating or exploring?

Envision the legacy you hope to leave. Write with detail about your life's purpose and what success looks like in this context. These expressions of your soul's calling become guides.

Crafting Personal Intentions

Now distill your broader life purpose into specific intentions in major areas like relationships, health, career, and personal growth.

Frame intentions positively - "I am in vibrant physical health" vs "I lose weight." Write them present tense, as already manifested. Repeat often like mantras or affirmations to imprint them subconsciously.

Sharing Intentions with Supportive Community

Articulating intentions to a circle of allies helps anchor them externally. Share either in trusted conversation or writing.

Be specific - "I intend to start my own business this year." Ask for their encouragement as you take steps to align actions with intentions. Voice your vision; inner truths gain power when spoken.

Integrating Intentions into Daily Rituals

Regularly reflect on how to translate lofty intentions into daily practices and rituals. For the intention of financial freedom, that might mean reviewing budgets, visualizing wealth, or consulting mentors.

Intentions manifest through consistent small steps more than occasional grand gestures. Make intentions actionable through incremental progress.

Designing an Aligned Daily Routine

Your days should energize and move you steadily toward intentions. Audit how you spend time to ensure alignment.

Optimizing When You Are Most Productive

Note when in the day and week your energy and focus peak. Schedule your most challenging priorities for these periods and lighter tasks for lower energy times.

Beware productivity killers like checking email first thing in the morning. Do your most important work when you are freshest. Flow state emerges more easily.

Balancing Doing, Being, Learning

Ensure your schedule includes a balance of work, rest and growth. Is there time for moving your mission forward as well as contemplation, play and learning?

Ideally address each area daily - even small doses enrich the whole. For example, an hour of work, 30 minutes reading, 15 minutes exercising and meditating. Rhythm sustains you.

Leveraging Transitional Time

Rather than only associating productivity with major blocks of time, leverage moments of transition: waiting in line, your commute, morning routine.

Listen to educational podcasts driving. Review your calendar while drinking coffee. Even five minutes of intentionality multiples productivity. Value small pockets.

Curating Inspiring Media Consumption

Audit what informational sources you engage and when. Ensure your podcasts, books, news consumption, etc. nourish your growth rather than simply entertain.

Set guidelines around limiting time sinks of distraction. Curiate a steady diet of ideas energizing your intentions. Garbage in, garbage out, but quality in, quality out. Feed mind and spirit.

Maintaining Accountability

Commit your routine intentions to paper or share them with an accountability partner for additional motivation. Keep notes on how well you adhere to your planned alignment.

Review inconsistencies without judgment, only adjusting and clarifying your goals. Steady progress, not perfection, is the aim. Consistent effort accumulates into transformation.

Integrating Mindfulness Practices

Mindfulness meditation cultivates non-judgmental presence, the foundation for clear inner guidance. Make it a pillar in your day.

Establishing a Daily Practice

Commit to a consistent formal sit of 10-20 minutes once or twice daily. Set reminders. Dedicate a quiet space. Start simply following the breath before exploring techniques.

Reframe busyness as resistance to slowing down. Carve out time for stillness consciously. Slip mindfulness into little moments too - waiting in line, at a red light, before picking up your phone.

Noticing Judgments During Meditation

In meditation, observe thoughts but don't engage them. Note judgments about your practice arising - "This isn't working," "I'm bad at this," etc.

Then gently return to the breath. Allowing judgments without following them reduces their power. Just witness then come back to presence.

Expanding Mindfulness Throughout Your Day

Gradually extend mindful presence beyond formal sitting to routine activities. Wash dishes, cook, exercise with full engagement.

When emotions or distractions arise, pause, breathe and redirect attention with compassion. Make mindfulness a way of moving through life rather than isolated practice.

journaling for Clarity

Journaling flushes mental chatter onto paper, clarifying emotions and untangling knotty problems.

Write stream-of-consciousness without censoring. Then read back reflectively to integrate pieces of yourself. Journal to process and organize thoughts, gain self-knowledge, solve challenges through new angles. Externalizing inner contents provides perspective.

Optimizing Work & Productivity

Align work to enliven rather than drain you. Apply consciousness to tasks to prevent drudgery and burnout.

Reframing Resistance

Notice when you procrastinate or avoid certain work. Often resistance masks fear - of failure, the unknown, imperfection, or envy at colleagues' success.

Shine light on resistance's root. Then reframe difficulties as opportunities to develop grit, humility, and trust in your abilities. Growth lives outside comfort zones. Breathe through fears and proceed.

Removed Distractions & Interruptions

Preserve intervals of deep focus on challenging projects by silencing devices, closing tabs, turning off notifications.

Schedule email in contained batches rather than continuously. Let people know when you will be offline. The brain requires long stretches of unfragmented attention to access flow state and creativity. Protect this space.

Working in Alignment with Energy

Hovering over work when energy is low breeds frustration. Instead, sync tasks with your body's optimal rhythms.

Do analytical work when mental acuity peaks, phone calls when voice is energetic, physical activity when restless. Your natural ebbs and flows want to support productivity. Observe them, then adapt.

Curating Inspiring Work Environments

Since environment impacts performance, craft energizing work spaces. Add plants, natural light, candles, vision boards with affirmations/goals, artwork, scents invoking focus.

Play enlivening music. Hoard snacks boosting concentration like nuts and dried fruit. Make spaces you wish never to leave by suffusing them with your spirit.

Maintaining Health & Wellbeing

Straying from self-care sabotages effectiveness. Prioritize renewal in order to thrive.

Honoring Your Emotional Needs

Work often suppresses emotions affecting performance - frustration, inadequacy, resentment. Create space to feel.

Vent privately through journaling or calls with trusted ears. Allow tears. Take breathers when tense. Providing release prevents emotions from hijacking progress. Manage your inner world skillfully.

Balancing Drivenness with Rest

Periodically examine your ratio of output versus input. Are you overly attached to relentless doing at the cost of being?

Carefully calibrate hustle and flow with ample rest to prevent burnout. Sabbaticals, weekends off, vacations, morning routines centered on self-care, all nourish sustainability. Balance receptivity and progress.

Maintaining Physical Health

The body is your vehicle for enacting purpose. How well are you caring for it? Assess your diet, activity and sleep. Make incremental improvements.

Food is foundational. Incorporate more vegetables, lean proteins, nuts, seeds and fruit. Hydrate with water and herbal tea. Move daily, stretch, strengthen, breathe deeply. Protect sleep sanctity. Listen to your body's whispers.

Developing Emotional Maturity

Success requires honest self-appraisal and ownership of inner terrain - fears, weaknesses, triggers, traumas. Do the inner work.

Unpack imposter syndrome projections, childhood wounds driving overcompensation, lessons from past failures. Achievement without

self-awareness breeds destruction. Growth flows from practicing
deep wisdom.

Defining Success Holistically

Some visions of "success" uplift and fulfill, others deplete and
isolate. Carefully define it for yourself based on your values.

Assessing Material Ambitions

If definitions of success revolve around status, possessions or
money, recalibrate them. These provide temporary highs often
ending in emptiness.

What priceless inner rewards beyond the material are you
neglecting? How can you feel successful on a soul level? Service,
love, growth and truth are lasting treasures.

Balancing Three Key Areas

Aim for balance between pursuing:

- **Financial** - sufficient resources to live without constant
  stress. But avoid over-prioritizing wealth for its own sake.

- **Relational** - meaningful connections with others. But avoid
  compromising values or losing yourself in relationships.

- **Personal** - self-actualization through developing your gifts
  and purpose. But avoid narcissism.

Integrate all three for fulfillment. Imbalance breeds discontent.

Curating Community & Support Systems

Humans require communal bonds. Seek out kindred spirits who
stimulate growth, offer empathy and wisdom, and share your values.

Build community through meaningful service, collaborations,
spiritual groups, and mentorship. We travel farthest accompanied by
the right companions. Cherish these soul ties.

Defining Your Unique Metrics

Rather than traditional markers like title, salary or awards, define personal success metrics aligned with your values.

These could include cultivating daily peace, creating art, raising compassionate children, realizing passions, maintaining integrity, leaving an ethical legacy. Write your own definition.

Embracing the Journey

Walking the path with heart is a process of continual surrender, not a final destination. What matters most is your deepening presence along the way.

Releasing Attachment to Specific Outcomes

Hold goals and visions lightly, as intentions not absolutes. Making happiness contingent on specific outcomes guarantees disappointment since life follows no script.

Stay open to possibilities taking different shapes than you imagined. Trust in unseen forces directing your purpose. Live in process.

Staying Present to Each Step

Reattach when your mind jumps ahead to the next milestone. Fully honor the necessary stage you are passing through now.

Each phase of growth has beauty and wisdom to savor. Resist rushing. Time is abundant for the patient heart. Breathe deeply and plunge into the experience before you.

Maintaining Beginner's Mind

However solid your knowledge, retain beginner's receptivity. Assume you have everything left to learn. Empty your cup often.

Avoid rigid ideas about who you are or how life works. Return regularly to not-knowing. The student's mindset propels progress. Never become too certain.

Letting Go of Outcomes

Surrender finally the insistence life meet your specific expectations. Relax into trust that each experience brings you exactly what you need for growth.

When faced with disappointment, search for the hidden blessings and lessons. There are no wrong turns, only unexpected wisdom. Your soul charted this course long before you were born. All is well.

And so we arrive at the journey's end, but only to embark again on a new ascent. The path has no terminus, though your footfalls grow more surefooted having walked this loop. You know the way now in your bones and sinews. This road is yours, wherever it leads. Stay true to the truth that fuels your purpose. Let your light shine.

Conclusion

We have now journeyed together through inner landscapes of shadow and light. I hope these words have provided mirrored compass points guiding you deeper into your truth. But in the end, your path is your own. What now matters most is the wisdom you choose to carry forward.

An Ongoing Journey

Self-discovery is not a finite process but rather an endless spiral, always inviting us into greater understanding and embodiment of truth. We never reach a static state of total enlightenment.

Rather than viewing this work as completed, see it as the foundation for the rest of your lifelong path of awakening. Consider this book a sturdy walking stick or pack of provisions for the road ahead. The journey has scarcely begun.

Committing to Continuous Growth

The temptation upon finishing a journey is to plant our feet and sightsee. But avoid complacency. Recall the fullest joy came not from reaching peaks, but in pushing upward through new horizons.

Commit now to stay devoted to continuous learning, self-examination and tangible progress. Measure "success" not through any crowning achievement but through persistently walking in alignment and deepening presence.

Carry forward everything that empowered understanding - meditation, journaling, community, time in nature, creative expression. Only consistent practice cultivates wisdom. Walk on.

Appreciating the Adventure

The mind conditioned by ego believes life's purpose is reaching a destination of fame, wealth, status. Thus it resists being present. Each moment is just fuel for getting to some better future place.

But infuse each step of your adventure with wonder. Even when the path feels steep or monochrome, find beauty in continuing to put one foot in front of the other with integrity. Fulfillment comes through practice, not achievement.

Living by Your Inner Authority

You possess now the light of expanded self-knowledge. Let this lamp guide you rather than external authorities pressuring you to conform.

Your inner voice, once but a whisper drowned by others' demands, has strengthened into steadfast wisdom. Trust and follow it, not the clamoring crowd. You know your truth. Stand firmly in it.

Welcoming More Light

If inner exploration has revealed your shadows, do not despair. There are further depths of radiance awaiting revelation if you continue diving.

Grace emerges from patience, compassion and openness in excavating truths slowly, without judgment. Believe that a part of you already dwells in this light. You need only unveil it.

Relinquishing Limiting Beliefs

Inspect again any remaining inner beliefs keeping you small - that wealth and spirituality cannot coexist, you must always struggle, the world will never improve.

Begin expanding beyond thought prisons you have outgrown. Every life circumstance you perceive as limited contains secret passageways inviting you to transcend it through faith. Move forward boldly.

Discovering Life's Hidden Invitation

Know that behind each challenge, frustration, loss and injustice lies an initiation guiding you to discover some new strength or wisdom within yourself.

With openness, you begin seeing difficulties as portals through which your highest self emerges. If you feel blocked in some area, turn inward for the locked door awaiting your key.

Continuing Your Shadow Work

The journey within is really a lifelong process of shadow integration. Do not shy from the necessary path of befriending and transmuting your darkness.

There are an infinite number of jewels hiding in those unexplored caves within. What you resist persists, so meet it with courage. Keep venturing beneath the surface toward wholeness.

Anchoring Your Growth

Transformation requires anchoring insights into your body and life practices, not just intellect. Keep co-creating outer forms that fortify and reflect inner shifts.

This means enacting consistent rituals - meditations, journaling, time in nature, exercise. It also means reshaping your environment, relationships and work to align with emerging wisdom. Embody each epiphany.

Serving as a Guidepost

You now hold navigational wisdom and experience for those just embarking on their inner odyssey. Offer it through writing, conversations, community leadership or mentorship.

Your hard-won capability for holding space for darkness allows others to accept their shadows. Your light can reflect the path for others. Let your gains ripple outward.

I hope these suggestions encourage continued momentum in your sacred quest for self-illumination. May your unfolding bring tidal waves of light to every shore. This is my prayer for you, voyager. Keep shining.

About the Author

With a voice that blends psychological insight and spiritual wisdom, Dr. Monday Farouq guides readers through the winding trails and hidden caverns of self-discovery in his transformative book "The Journey Inward: Discovering Your Own Truth."

As a psychologist and rehabilitation specialist, Dr. Farouq's extensive clinical experience provides a unique lens for illuminating the mind-body connection along the path to profound understanding and healing. His background in rehabilitation shapes his holistic approach of integrating physical, emotional and spiritual components on the journey toward inner peace and life purpose.

Dr. Farouq's book transcends traditional self-help, weaving together storytelling, metaphors, clinical perspectives and contemplative practices into a rich tapestry. His words offer signposts for navigating the adventures and obstacles that arise along the road of awakening.

Beyond his accomplished work as an author, Dr. Farouq is known for his warmth and wisdom guiding patients through deep personal transformations in his therapy practice. His commitment to continuous learning echoes throughout his writing, reminding readers that self-discovery is a lifelong process, not a single destination.

With care and nuance, Dr. Farouq provides keys that assist individuals in unlocking their inner truths, while also acknowledging the mysterious nature of the soul's unfolding. He empowers readers to trust their own inner voices and live with authenticity aligned with personal values.

As both a knowledgeable guide and fellow sojourner, Dr. Monday Farouq walks alongside readers in their sacred quest for self-knowledge and empowerment. With compassion and insight, he invites us all to embrace the journey within.

www.ingramcontent.com/pod-product-compliance
Lightning Source LLC
Chambersburg PA
CBHW071109260726
48661CB00006B/2557